Robert Paterson

The American Sabbath

A sermon

Robert Paterson

The American Sabbath
A sermon

ISBN/EAN: 9783743326774

Manufactured in Europe, USA, Canada, Australia, Japa

Cover: Foto ©ninafisch / pixelio.de

Manufactured and distributed by brebook publishing software
(www.brebook.com)

Robert Paterson

The American Sabbath

THE

AMERICAN SABBATH.

PHILADELPHIA:

PRESBYTERIAN BOARD OF PUBLICATION,

No. 821 CHESTNUT STREET.

THE AMERICAN SABBATH.

"Thus the heavens and the earth were finished, and all the host of them. And on the seventh day God ended his work which he had made; and he rested on the seventh day from all his work which he had made. And God blessed the seventh day and sanctified it; because that in it he had rested from all his work which God created and made."—Genesis ii. 1–4.

Law is naturally repulsive. It offends our native independence to submit our wills to the will of another. For law demands submission before one knows the reason for it. Indeed, this is the difference between law and persuasion, that law assumes the inability of many of the people to comprehend the reasons of enactments, and the necessity of obedience without such knowledge. Hence the majority of every community, women, children, etc., are not consulted in the making of laws, and

even the voters repose the trust of legislation
in the hands of statesmen supposed to be wiser
on this subject than those who have not studied
law.   In monarchical countries laws are made
with even less reference to the will of those
who shall obey them.   In the kingdom of
heaven, where the highest perfection of
wisdom exists in the Lawgiver, and especially
in the law given to the human race in its in-
fancy, there is no question raised as to man's
willingness to submit to the divine commands.
But, inasmuch as all true obedience is voluntary, our divine Lawgiver takes the most
effectual means of inducing our cheerful consent by giving us his Sabbath law embodied
in the most cogent form of his own example
of labour and rest.   By this example the Creator
has given the law of the Sabbath to all his
creatures—not to the Jewish nation merely,
which did not exist for centuries afterwards—
but to Adam and all his posterity; and not
to the human race alone, but to all other
orders of beings composed of material bodies
and rational souls, in all worlds acquainted

with this divine example.   The sons of God, who shouted for joy on the completion of the newest world of God's ancient universe, were as much instructed by this divine example of alternate labour and repose as Adam.   There is no other right of humanity chartered to us by such a sacred sanction.   Neither the sacredness of property, nor of life, nor of marriage, is sheltered under the glorious Shekinah of that divine example, which glorifies the day of sacred rest.   But lest it might seem too great a presumption for man to enter into this divine Sabbatism, it is added, "and God blessed the seventh day and sanctified it" —set it apart from common to sacred uses, and made it an occasion of bestowing his blessing on those who thus observed it.   The divine institution of a seventh day of sacred rest after six days of labour is here declared to be coeval with the human race, and a God-given right of all men.   I am aware that this is denied by some, who allege that the Sabbath was a purely Jewish institution, unknown to men before the exodus of Israel,

1 *

and therefore bound up with the fortunes of that people, and vanishing like their other local and national usages. They endeavour to evade this text by alleging that Moses wrote proleptically; that is, that he made a mistake in narrating God's rest at this period; that there was no such rest as here narrated; that the whole narrative of the six days' work of creation is contradicted by modern science; and that there is no mention of the observance of the Sabbath in the subsequent history till the exodus.

I shall not here enter on the question of the truth of Moses' account of the creation of all things in the beginning, and the subsequent and distinct work of the making of this world into a habitable abode for man in the six days of the Mosaic narrative, which are both narrated in my text—created and made. With the empty *theories* of scientific men we have here nothing to do; but I allege that no *fact* of science has been proved to contradict the Books of Moses. I make this assertion, not rashly, but after twenty-five years' observation of the progress of the physical sciences, and an examination of all the alleged anti-biblical facts of Astronomy, Physical Geography, Physiology, Ethnology, Phrenology, Geology, and Historical Criticism. No man has yet established any *fact* of science contradictory of the Bible narrative. Misrepresentations of the Bible and misrepresentations of science we have in great abundance; but no proof that Moses lied. Till this is proved we accept Moses' account as true. The account he gives us here is, that God rested on the seventh day. He repeats the statement in the Fourth Commandment. This fact would be no more weakened by the subsequent neglect of mankind to imitate God's example of Sabbath-keeping, if that was the fact, than by their neglect of any other part of a holy life. The authority of a divine example and institution depends not on man's obedience. This alleged neglect of the patriarchs to observe the Sabbath is not proved. The omission of any notice of their observance of such a tranquil institution by Moses, in his brief notices of the most remarkable events of a period of near three thousand years, is no proof of their omission of its observance.

But the allegation of the omission of reference to this institution is incorrect. There are many references to it, all the more emphatic that they are not formal, but incidental. To what else are we to trace the sacredness of the number seven?—a sacredness recognized by God himself, when he says, "vengeance shall be taken on Cain's murderer seven-fold," *i. e.* a vengeance which, having fully satisfied itself, brings rest to the soul. Why should the beasts designed for sacrifice come into the ark by sevens? Whence the arrangement of the years of famine and plenty in Egypt by sevens? To what else can the seven days of the Passover week refer? All this is not mere human invention; it is God's speech; it is God's symbolism. But it would have been unintelligible to man without the previous consecration of the week of seven days; with that institution in existence, it is perfectly plain and natural. Such a week was well known to Noah. God said to him, "Yet seven days and I will cause it to rain on the earth." Noah sends out his raven and his dove after intervals of seven days. Laban and Jacob were well acquainted with the week. Job's friends sat down to comfort him seven days. Joseph mourned for his father seven days. The prevalence of the week of seven days, and of the dedication of the seventh day to the worship of the chief deity among the various nations of the earth, proves its antiquity. Thus, the Greeks and Romans, and natives of Western Asia, and our own ancestors, dedicated that day to the sun. From China to Peru, the division of time into weeks attests the ancient and common origin of the institution, and refutes those who maintain that the Sabbath is a purely Jewish institution.

1. The Sabbath then *is a primeval and catholic institution.* For the example of God is not only the highest authority; it is also of the most universal and perpetual influence, inasmuch as it indicates that Sabbath rest is

founded in the very nature bestowed upon us by our Creator, and in the relations which he sustains to us. The right to labour six days, and to rest the seventh, is here represented as a natural, inalienable right of man, bestowed on him by his Creator, and fenced in by the most sacred sanctions of religion.

I am perfectly warranted, then, in taking as the subject of this discourse, not the Jewish Sabbath, which was a national institution, nor the Christian Sabbath, which is a religious privilege; but the natural right of any man, and of every man, without respect to his nationality or to his religion, to rest from labour on the weekly Sabbath. I allege that the Chinese, and the Hindoo, and the Mohammedan, and the infidel, no less than the Jew or the Christian, have here the declaration of a God-given right to rest one day in seven, of which no man may deprive them, and of which men may no more deprive themselves than they may deprive themselves of their God-given rights to life and liberty. And since this glorious American Union admits to its privileges every child of our common Father, not to rob him of his God-given rights, but to protect him in their enjoyment, to throw around the weak and the ignorant the mantle of loving protection and lawful power derived from the great Law-giver (for there is no power but of God), and since, with common consent, since the beginning of our Republic, our people, our legislators, our judges, our governors, and our presidents, from George Washington to Abraham Lincoln, have publicly vindicated the people's right to the weekly day of sacred rest, it is proper to designate it the American Sabbath.

The attempt is now being made to procure a reversal of this national acknowledgment of the Sabbath ; to repeal the laws forbidding common labour on that day, and thus to make it a purely religious institution, like the sacraments, to be observed by those who desire to observe it, and to be disregarded by others. The proposal, indeed, is not in so many words to abolish Sabbath rest and recreation;

it is, in words, a proposal to allow a large portion of the people to spend the day in revelry as a day of amusement; but, in order to do this, it is found necessary to repeal the law forbidding common labour, because amusement even cannot be carried on without common labour. The saloon-keeper must labour in his vocation, and the stoker, and the conductor, and the brakesman, and the engine-driver, and the steamboat crew, and the musicians, and the confectioner, and the milliner, and the hair-dresser, and the washerwoman, the circus troupe, the dancers, and the actors and actresses, and all the host of amusement-makers, must labour very hard for the recreation of the rest of the people on Sabbath. But it would be manifestly absurd to suppose that the rum-seller, and the gambler, and the actor should enjoy a liberty for their vocations denied to the printer, or to the carpenter, or the butcher, or to any other honest labourer. If it is lawful for these demoralizing professions to ply their crafts on the Sabbath, it is much more lawful for the mechanic to do an honest day's work. The Liquor Dealers' Associations perceive the force of this argument, and, accordingly, they ask a repeal of the law forbidding common labour on Sabbath. They allege that the law is now violated by multitudes, but that its existence is some hindrance to general Sabbath-breaking, and, therefore, they ask its repeal. They began, seven years ago, by asserting Sunday revelry, and now they demand Sunday labour. The tree bears its proper fruit. All experience shows that the Sabbath rest from labour has never been enjoyed by any people who spent the day in revelry. The sense of the sacredness of this as a divine institution, a God-given right, lies at the basis of the enjoyment of its privileges. Wherever these sanctions have been removed there is no rest for the people on Sabbath. Competition in business would soon compel tradesmen and mechanics to work seven days in the week, were the Sabbath law repealed. The desire for the abolition of the law forbidding Sabbath labour

2

is, then, simply a desire to compel seven days' labour every week.

Let it be distinctly understood that the Sabbath laws of these States simply forbid common labour, the keeping open of tippling-houses, and any rout or sport which disturbs any congregation of worshippers on the Sabbath. The law does not say that any man shall go to this church, or to that church, or to any church; that he shall stay in his house, or read his Bible, or sing hymns, or hear sermons; that he shall not eat a good dinner if he can get it, nor drink beer, nor smoke, nor read newspapers or novels, nor hear music, if he is so inclined. The civil law does not forbid social parties, nor card-playing, nor dancing, nor gymnastics, either in the house or in the field, provided, only, that no congregation is disturbed at worship by such revelry. I am not now commending such a mode of spending the Sabbath, nor stating what *God's* law says on the subject. I am stating the law of the State—a law which certainly infringes no man's liberty of conscience, and which leaves the broadest room for every kind of recreation compatible with the preservation of the labourer's day of rest, at all. Less than this the Commonwealth cannot do without abnegation of its right to preserve the lives of its people.

2. The Sabbath rest *is necessary to preserve the lives of the people.* The law of periodicity controls every known substance in the universe. It is seen in the full change and quarters of the moon, in the rising and setting of the sun, in the orbit of the earth, in the consequent succession of day and night, and of spring, summer, autumn, and winter; in the inspiration and expiration of our breath, in the relaxation and contraction of our muscles, in the alternations of labour and repose which are thus necessitated. Not only man—the brute creation, and even inanimate things, are subject to this law. No substance can endure eternal motion. Even the winds must sometimes rest. A bar of iron continually hammered, even with the slightest force, will become first hard as steel,

then brittle as glass, and eventually fly into fragments. The superintendent of the North-western Railway of England reports, after tabulating the performance of over twelve hundred locomotives and a corresponding number of trains for many years, that the continual, unresting working of a locomotive so crystallizes the axles that dangerous and costly accidents from sudden fracture necessarily result; that it is necessary to allow these machines a day's rest in the week;—an emphatic testimony coming from a Sabbath-breaking railroad.

The law of periodical rest applies to all working animals. Bianconi, the celebrated Irish car proprietor, calculates that his horses will run eight miles an hour for six days in the week better than six miles an hour for seven days in the week, and that there is thus a saving of thirteen per cent. of animal life by allowing them to rest on Sabbath; adding, "I am persuaded that man cannot be wiser than his Maker." On the question of endurance, it is now settled that

horses which become exhausted in omnibus
and street-car work with five and a half
years of Sunday labour will last eight years
of six-day labour. It is thus a demonstrated
fact of natural history that working animals
need not only a nightly repose, but also a
weekly rest from labour; and that if deprived
of this weekly rest their lives are shortened.
In short, seven-day work is killing work for
the horse or the ox. It is worthy of note
that this fact was known to the Author of
the Sabbath, who therefore commanded that
the ox and the ass should rest on Sabbath as
well as men. Were there no other ground
for its existence, the prevention of cruelty to
animals would be a sufficient justification of
the Sabbath law.

When we come to inquire whether the
human body is subject to the same laws of
physiology which regulate the preservation
of all other animals, physiologists assure us
that man is no exception to the universal law
of periodicity of labour and of rest; that the
law of rest is as imperative as the law of food

2 *

or the law of breath; that the nightly repose does not restore the balance of the system; that continuous mental labour ends in idiocy or insanity, and unbroken bodily labour in premature old age or sudden death; and that the weekly rest of the Sabbath is necessary to the preservation of life. The testimonies to this effect are too numerous to be transcribed. I shall only quote a few leading American and British authorities, and this will be sufficient, since there is no contradictory testimony. The medical profession is as unanimous in asserting the necessity of the Sabbath's rest to the working man's life as in asserting his need of air or food.

Dr. Parre, after many years' practice in London, gave the following sworn testimony before a committee of the House of Commons:

" All men, of whatever class, who must necessarily be occupied six days in the week, should abstain on the seventh; and in the course of life would assuredly gain by giving to their bodies the repose, and to their minds the change of ideas, suited to the day for which it was appointed by heavenly wisdom. I have frequently observed the death of medical men from continued exertion. I have advised the clergyman, in lieu of his Sabbath, to rest one day in the week; it forms a continual prescription of mine. I have seen many destroyed by their duties on that day; and to preserve them I have frequently suspended them for a season from the discharge of their duties. The working of the mind in one continuous train of thought is destructive of life in the most distinguished class of society, and senators themselves stand in need of reform in that particular. I have observed many of them destroyed by neglecting this economy of life."

The labouring classes, as we might expect, are no less in need of rest. Six hundred and forty-one London physicians unite their testimony to the necessity of the Sabbath in a petition to Parliament against legalizing Sabbath desecration. They say:

" Your petitioners, from their acquaintance with the labouring classes and with the laws which regulate the human economy, are convinced that a seventh day of rest, instituted by God and coeval with the existence of man, is essential to the bodily health and mental vigour of men in every station of life."

Of American physiologists, Carpenter, in his letter to Granger, says:

" My own experience is very strong as to the importance of complete rest and change of thought once in the week."

Dr. Mussey, in a formal physiological exposition of the subject, declares:

" Under the due observance of the Sabbath, life would, on the average, be prolonged more than one-seventh of the whole period; that is, more than seven years in fifty."

Statistics prove that the loss of life by Sabbath drudgery and general toil is as much as fifty per cent. in England among the working classes; the average town life of gentlemen being forty-two, of labourers, twenty-one years; in the country, gentlemen fifty, labourers thirty-five years. Increase of rest is increase of life to the worker.

The State, then, has the same right to protect the Sabbath rest of the people by law as she has to protect their lives. The same reason which authorizes the prevention and removal of nuisances injurious to the health and dangerous to the lives of the citizens—though they may be profitable to certain classes—authorizes the suppression of Sabbath labour. Sabbath labour, cutting short human life more than one-seventh, as six hundred and fifty physicians testify, would be equivalent to three hundred murders yearly in Chicago alone. Has not the State a right to prevent three hundred murders?

It may be said that this labour is voluntary on the part of the Sabbath drudges. It is mockery to call the compulsion of necessity voluntary. But suppose it were voluntary; has any man a right to commit suicide? Is it not the highest crime known to our laws? Has not the State a right to arrest a man contemplating self-destruction, and to prevent the crime? And if his crime contemplates not only injury to his own life, but the injury of his neighbour's life also, has not the State the right to prevent that injury? Why not as well say that a man has a right to import cholera or yellow fever?

3. The State *has the right to prevent crime and to forbid provocations thereto.* Hence the very common prohibition by our legislatures of keeping open taverns on election day, and the insertion of clauses in the charters of colleges forbidding the sale of liquor in their vicinity, and the prohibition of the sale of lottery tickets. Sunday drinking has been demonstrated by long experience to be a fruitful nursery of crime. Take, for example, the experience of New York during this year, 1867—a year of Sabbath rest—and the past years of Sunday revelry. In 1859 the grand jury made the following presentment: "The grand jury cannot close their labours without presenting to the court and to the public the important fact that a very large portion of the business which has occupied

its attention has arisen from the sale and use
of intoxicating liquors. Nearly all the cases
for murder and assault and battery which
have been investigated (and the number is
great) have been found to spring from that
cause." From the records of the prisons, it
appears that of the twenty-seven thousand
eight hundred and forty-five commitments to
prison in New York in 1857, twenty-three
thousand eight hundred and seventeen were
persons of intemperate habits, and of these
nine thousand seven hundred and twenty-six
were females. More than five-sixths of the
criminals had their training in the saloons,
and more than one-third of the whole number were drunken women! No wonder the
grand jury says, "With very few exceptions,
the crimes charged have their origin in re-
sorts and dens of iniquity, where intoxicating
liquors are sold and drank." The sale and
consumption of liquor on Sabbath, and the
resulting drunkenness and crime, are double
those of other days, in consequence of the
much greater number of men released from

work. On four Sundays in April, 1866, before the closing of the liquor-shops under the new Excise law, the number of arrests was five hundred and eighty-three; on four Sundays in May, when they were closed, the arrests were reduced to two hundred and fifty-seven—a reduction of three hundred and twenty-six, or over four thousand per annum! Will any one venture to assert that legislators overstep their province in preventing four thousand crimes per annum?

The chaplain of Clerkenwell prison testified before the British House of Commons: "I do not recollect a single case of capital offence where the party had not been a Sabbath-breaker. Indeed, I may say in reference to prisoners of all classes, that in nineteen cases out of twenty they have not only neglected the Sabbath, but all religious ordinances." Of the one hundred thousand criminals under his care during eighteen years, he testified that "the leading causes of crime had been impatience of parental restraint, violation of the Sabbath, evil associations, especially with abandoned females, and drunkenness arising from attending public-houses and beer-gardens;" the very associations and institutions which the Liquor Dealers' Associations are now labouring to foster by the repeal of Sabbath laws. The law-abiding people have the right to restrain these men from making criminals, and from burdening us with the enormous costs of penitentiaries and officers. The prevention of crime is the very first design of law.

In the year in which the act was passed closing public houses on Sabbath throughout Scotland, a bill was, in the same session of Parliament, brought in and passed on behalf of the municipal authorities of Edinburgh, to enable them to raise and charge on the inhabitants of that city a sum of twelve thousand pounds for enlarging the jail, which had been found wholly insufficient for the number of offenders in that locality. Both bills, having passed, came into operation at the end of the session, and the public-houses were closed on Sabbaths, which was attended

3

with such success that it was found by the end of the year that the number of criminal offences in the city was reduced by one-third. The municipal authorities, finding this result, refrained for a time from raising the twelve thousand pounds authorized by the act; and finding subsequently that the number of offences was still further reduced, they gave up the thought of enlarging the jail or of raising the money authorized to be assessed for that purpose, whereby the citizens escaped the heavy charge which would have been laid on them; and now, after the lapse of several years, that jail, which was before so insufficient for the large number of prisoners to be crowded into it, is so much too large for the reduced number requiring to be confined there that actually one wing of it is entirely vacant, the authorities are considering to what purpose that wing shall be applied, and it is proposed to apply it for an asylum for females reduced to a state of debility by former excess and intoxication.

4. The Sabbath *is necessary to the preser-*

vation of our republican institutions. Government is based on the social nature of man, and contemplates him as a member of society. Now, society implies a willingness on the part of its individual members to restrain their natural selfishness for the general benefit. Government, however, supposes some degree of unwillingness and selfishness, and the necessity of suppressing it by force;—jails, penitentiaries, armies, all attest the need of force. The greater the amount of selfishness in a community, the greater the force necessary to suppress it. Hence the maxim, "a degraded people and a strong government;" meaning thereby a powerful army. Ignorance is the mother and nurse of selfishness. The more ignorant the man, the more passionate and self-willed. The first step towards civil government is self-government, and that is a process of education. Let any class of men be deprived of opportunities of education, and kept constantly occupied in daily labour, their native animal instincts, uncorrected by education, will so develop themselves that they will become selfish, sensual, vicious and brutish. They can only be governed by force of arms and fear of punishment. Five millions of soldiers are required now to preserve the peace of Europe. A vicious people necessitates a despotic government. No man would dream of a republican form of government for the penitentiary. Even where ignorance has not developed into vice, we realize the fact that it is a disqualification for the exercise of government, and refuse children the exercise of the ballot. Intelligence and virtue are the fundamental requirements of a republican government. If the people of any country are ignorant and vicious, a republican form of government is an impracticable absurdity there. The experience of Greece, of Rome, of France, of Mexico, has satisfied all reflecting minds of this fact.

But continuous labour forbids popular intelligence. The great majority of mankind must labour with their hands for daily bread; this is the law of heaven, and such is the

observed fact. Their daily labour is always
so prolonged that little or no time, and less
disposition, to prosecute mental labour remain
after the fatigues of the day. Very few of
the labouring classes ever obtain anything
more than the rudiments of an education in
their childhood—the power of reading and
writing—by which they may acquire necessary information in after life, if they can
have opportunity to use it, and will make
the attempt. But if they are compelled to
toil seven days in the week, they can have no
such opportunity, and must continue mere
animals, without any capacity for learning
their rights or their duties as citizens, or the
motives by which they should be influenced
to love their neighbours as themselves. And
this mental degradation reacts again on the
animal frame, and promotes filth and fever.
We have unfortunately an abundance of
practical demonstrations of this principle in
the European emigrants who now come to
our shores to escape the miseries of the degradation of the people there. Imagine a New

3 *

England Puritan taking off his hat to a land-
lord, or paying taxes to an Episcopal church,
or asking my Lord Somebody's leave to fish
in the river!

The Sabbath law gives the time necessary
for the education of the working man. It
affords him a weekly opportunity of culti-
vating his powers of thought, of cherishing
the family and social affections, of considering himself something more than a working
machine, or than an eating and drinking
animal, or than the born serf and ploughman
of a landed proprietor, or the drudge of a
capitalist. It affords the opportunity, if he
will use it, of considering the most elevating
subjects of thought, and of studying the most
attractive examples of heroism, patriotism
and benevolence under the most advantageous
circumstances.

The eminent physiologist, Draper—whom
no one who has read his various, learned
and Rationalistic writings will accuse of any
leanings towards Puritanism—bears the following emphatic and eloquent testimony to

the intellectual and social influence of the Sabbath :

"Out of the numberless blessings which have thus been conferred on our race by the Church, the physiologist may be permitted to select one for remark, which in an eminent manner has contributed to our physical and moral well-being: It is the institution of the Sabbath day. Not that this originated with, or is peculiar to, the Christian faith, since, as is known to all, it dates from the remotest times, and was directly adopted from the Hebrew ceremonial. Its sanctification and enforcement by the Church was at once an object important in the highest degree in ecclesiastical polity and a boon to all classes of men; for, in whatever position in life we may be placed, it is needful for us to have an opportunity of rest. No man can for any length of time pursue one avocation or one train of thought without mental, and therefore bodily, injury—nay, without insanity. The constitution of the brain is such that it must have its time of repose. Periodicity is stamped upon it.   Nor is it enough that it is awake and in action by day, and in the silence of night obtains rest and repose; that same periodicity which belongs to it as a whole belongs to all its constituent parts. One portion of it cannot be called into incessant action without the risk of injury.   Its different regions, devoted to different functions, must have their separate times of rest. The excitement of one part must be coincident with a pause in the action of another. It is not possible for mental equilibrium to be maintained with one idea or one monotonous mode of life.   There is a necessity even for men of great intellectual endowments, whose minds are often strained to the utmost, to fall back on other pursuits; and thus it will always be that one seeks refuge in the pleasures of quiet country life, another in foreign travel, another in social amusements.   Pitt sought a relaxation from the cares of politics in the excitement of the chase.   Davy found a relief and consolation in the rod and line.   And among

men whose lot is cast in the lowest condition,
whose hard destiny it is to spend their whole
lives in the pursuit of their daily bread, with
one train of thought and one unvarying
course of events, the same principle impe-
riously applies. It is often said that the
pleasures of religion are wholly prospective,
and to be realized only in another world;
but in this there is a mistake, for those con-
solations commence even here, and temper
the bitterness of fate. The virtuous labourer,
though he may be ground down with the
oppressions of his social condition, is not without his relief; at the anvil, the loom, or even
the bottom of the mine, he is leading a double
existence; the miseries of the body find a
contrast in the calm of the soul; the warfare
without is compensated by the peace within;
the dark night of life here serves only to
brighten the glories of the prospect beyond.
Hope is the daughter of despair. And thus
a kind Providence so overrules events that it
matters not in what station we may be,
wealthy or poor, intellectual or lowly, a

refuge is always at hand, and the mind, worn out with one thing, turns to another, and its physical excitement is followed by physical repose. By the enforcement of the Sabbath the Church gave effect to this providential system of physical and mental relief. Her chief strength lay in this, that she concerned herself with the common man, who never in the world's history before had any to watch over or to care for him. She humanized him by the devotional solemnities of a sacred day —a day of entire relief from toil. Ignorant and rude though he might be, it was not possible for him to enter her hoary temples without being made a better man. The atmosphere of rest, the twilight streaming through the painted windows, the prayer in an unknown tongue—the slow chanting of old hymns, or the swelling forth of those noble strains of music which, once heard, are graven in remembrance for ever,—these she had made, with more than worldly wisdom, the elements or incidents of public worship. She gratified the manly sense by asserting before her altar the equality of all men, by making the vain and transitory gradations of society disappear, and by teaching the rich and the poor, the great and the humble, their common dependence on the mercy of God."

5. The State has a right to protect the Sabbath *as an essential part of the religion of the people.* Public worship is an indispensable part of that religion, and by common consent some common time must be allotted for it. In all Christian countries this is the same day which our State law protects. It is not necessary here to discuss the particular day of the week to be devoted to worship, as those with whom we now contend do not propose to change the day, but to abolish the Sabbath altogether, because it is a part of Christianity. We allege that for that very reason the State is bound to protect it.

The allegation that the State has no right to interfere with the Sabbath, because it is sanctioned by religion, is utterly unfounded. Religious sanctions are applicable to many of the affairs of civil life, which are not, on that account, outlawed by the legislature and jurisprudence of the republic. The oath, for instance, is a religious ordinance, an appeal to the Omniscient Judge of the living and the dead, instituted by God, and observed as a religious ordinance by all Christendom. Take away its religious character, and you take away all its influence and reduce it to a mere mockery. But shall we repeal all our legislation on the subject and cease to regard perjury as an aggravated crime, and declare the acts punishing it unconstitutional, because the oath is a religious ordinance, and the State has no right to meddle with religion? So, also, marriage is a divine ordinance, instituted at the same time as the Sabbath, given to the same persons, and, like that, enforced by religious sanctions. But shall we comply with the wish of infidel citizens to consider it, therefore, as a purely religious institution, entirely voluntary in its nature, and binding only so long as the consciences of the parties shall pronounce desirable, but no longer obligatory than they themselves shall choose? This is, indeed, the doctrine of many of the same parties who now urge the repeal of the Sabbath law and of all laws recognizing Christianity in any way. They would have the laws regulating marriage repealed, and all men and women left at liberty to make and annul such contracts at their pleasure. Petitions to this effect have been circulated in the State of New York; and probably we shall be soon asked to legalize Free Love under the same pleas—of relieving the courts, of promoting public morality, and of non-interference with conscience. The principle is the same in the one case as in the other. No man has any higher right to his wife or to his life than to his Sabbath. It is a God-given, inalienable right, fenced in by the highest of all sanctions. So far from the religious sanctions of the Sabbath forming a reason for expelling it from the protection of civil law, this sacred character constitutes the highest reason for such protection.

The Sabbath is that part of our common Christianity which brings before the people

4

those principles of religion upon which government is based, those supreme obligations to the All-seeing Disposer of life, upon a right regard to which all human law depends; for the sanctions of all human law are based upon the acknowledgment of the divine law by the people. Without this recognition of God's authority, the execution of a criminal could have no more weight than the slaughter of an ox, and an oath no more validity than a street peddler's proclamation. Hence, all governments, even among the heathen, have recognized the natural necessity of religion; and among all Christian people the Christian religion has, in one form or another, been embodied in their jurisprudence. Though no particular form of Christianity is exclusively recognized, and no sect is established and paid out of the public taxes, our government is not, therefore, irreligious. It is a great mistake to suppose that ours is an infidel government. In truth, an infidel government is impossible, as France has demonstrated by bloody experiment. Ours is a Christian government. In the fundamental document of our national character, the immortal Declaration of Independence, we explicitly recognized God as our Creator, and derived our rights to life, liberty, and the pursuit of happiness from him. We asserted the Christian idea of the equality of all men as a God-given right. We made our appeal to him as Supreme Ruler on the bench of justice of the world, and as our national Ruler, by the solemn sanction of the oath, and by the wager of battle, the decision of which in our favour gave us national existence. We established our government for the maintenance of these God-given rights to life, liberty, and the pursuit of happiness, and consequently for the maintenance of the Sabbath as essential to the life and liberty and happiness of the people. We refuse to acknowledge the right of any man or body of men to practice customs contrary to the morals of Christianity, even upon the plea of liberty of conscience. We allow no conscientious right of the Chinese to sell his daughters, as the religion of Confucius commands. We prohibit the Mohammedan from his conscientious duty of putting infidels to the sword. We will not legalize the Mormon's polygamy nor the Spiritualist's free love upon any plea of conscience. The Jew may not stone the false prophet or dreamer of dreams to death, according to the command of Moses. We refuse the infidel the right to establish his gambling hells, and we declare the sale of lottery tickets a crime punishable by law. We do all this because the governments of the United States of America are not Jewish governments, nor Mormon governments, nor Chinese governments, much less infidel governments, but Christian governments. Christianity is the basis of the common law of the land. All our jurisprudence is founded on Christian morality, and has been so from the very foundation of our nation. The Sabbath law is a part of our national Christianity, and the attempt to repeal it is part of a systematic attempt, on the part of infidels, to deprive our nation of its Christian character, to introduce the Red Republic, to make America what France was in the days of Danton and Robespierre, and the Reign of Terror. But the decisions of our courts, with entire unanimity, oppose this infidel attempt. Judge Story, Judge Kent, and indeed all who have had occasion to deliver judgment on the matter—in whatever State of those which enact the Sabbath law—have decided that the Sabbath law is a part of our national Christianity and of our common law.

The decision of the Supreme Court of New York, February Term, 1861, Justices Clerke, Sutherland and Allen, in the case of Gustav Lindenmüller vs. The People, convicted under the act of April, 1860, of giving dramatic representations on Sunday, very fully and ably sustains the constitutionality of Sunday laws. We quote a few sentences from the elaborate opinion, which is understood to be written by Judge Allen:

" As a civil and political institution, the establishment and regulation of a Sabbath is

4 *

within the just power of the civil government. Older than our government, the framers of the Constitution did not abolish, alter, or weaken its sanction, but recognized, as they might otherwise have established, it. All interests require national uniformity in the day observed, and that its observance should be so far compulsory as to protect those who desire and are entitled to the day.

"As a civil institution, the sanction of the day is at the option of the legislature; but it is fit that the Christian Sabbath should be observed by a Christian people, and it does not detract from the moral or legal sanction of a statute that it conforms to the law of God, as recognized by the great majority of the people. Existing here by common law, all that the legislature attempts to do is to regulate its observance. The common law recognizes the day; contracts, land redemption, etc., maturing on Sunday, must be performed on Saturday or Monday. Judicial acts on the Sabbath are mostly illegal.

Work done on Sunday cannot be recovered for, etc.

"The Christian Sabbath is, then, one of the civil institutions of the State, to which the business and duties of life are by the common law made to conform and adapt themselves. Nor is it a violation of the rights of conscience of any that the Sabbath of the people, immemorially enjoyed, sanctioned by common law, and recognized in the Constitution, should be respected and protected by the law-making power.

"The existence of the Sabbath as a civil institution being conceded, as it must be, the right of the legislature to control and regulate it and its observance is a necessary sequence. Precedents are found in the statutes of every government really or nominally Christian, from the period of Athelstan to the present day.

"Nearly all the States of the Union have passed laws against Sabbath-breaking, and prohibiting secular pursuits on that day; and in none have they been held repugnant to the Constitution, with the exception of California; while in most States, the legislature has been upheld by the courts and sustained by well-reasoned opinions.

" The act now complained of compels no religious observance, and offences against it are punishable not as sins against God, but as injurious to society. It rests upon the same foundation as a multitude of other statutes— such as those against gambling, lotteries, horse-racing, etc—laws which do restrain the citizen, and deprive him of some of his rights; but the legislature has the right to prohibit acts injurious to the public, subversive of the government, and which tend to the destruction of the morals of the people, and to disturb the peace and good order of society. It is exclusively for the legislature to determine what acts should be prohibited as dangerous to the community.

" It is the right of the citizen to be protected from offences against decency and against acts which tend to corrupt the morals and debase the moral sense of the community.

It is the right of the citizen that the Sabbath, as a civil institution, should be kept in a way not inconsistent with its purpose and the necessity out of which it grew as a day of rest, rather than as a day of riot and disorder, which would be to overthrow it and render it a curse rather than a blessing.

" But it is urged that it is the right of the citizen to regard the Sabbath as a day of innocent recreation and amusement. That is not innocent which may operate injuriously upon the morals of old or young, which tends to interrupt the quiet worship of the Sabbath, and which grievously offends the moral sense of the community, and thus tends to a breach of the peace. It may well be that the legislature thought that a Sunday theatre, with its drinking saloons and its usual inducements to licentiousness and other kindred vices, was not consistent with the peace, good order and safety of the city. They might well be of the opinion that such a place would be 'a nursery of vice, a school of preparation to qualify young men for the

gallows and young women for the brothel.'
But whatever the reason may have been, it
was a matter within the legislative discretion
and power, and their will must stand as the
reason of the law."

Judge Ludlow, of Pennsylvania, in the
case of Jeandelle, speaks the same language:

"Christianity has been decided to be a part
of the common law of Pennsylvania (Up-
degrave *vs.* The Commonwealth, 11 Serg &
Rawle, 394); and although it is so in a re-
stricted or modified sense, yet its divine
origin and truth are admitted; and therefore
it is not to be maliciously or openly resisted
and blasphemed against, to the annoyance of
believers or the injury of the public."

He then goes on to cite the legislation and
decisions of courts, all affirming the same
principle; among others, Chief Justice Lewis,
in The Commonwealth *vs.* Johnston:

"The Sabbath is a Christian institution,
recognized by the common law, and the Constitution, and on this ground alone have the

legislature a right to pass laws for its observance." (2 Am. Law Reg. 529.)

"By the common law of the Commonwealth, then, every citizen is entitled to enjoy the first day of the week in undisturbed quiet and repose, that he may exercise his 'natural and indefeasible right to worship Almighty God according to the dictates of his own conscience;' and whatever actual noise or disorder hinders seriously or destroys altogether this inestimable right is and always has been a breach of the peace." "The Sabbath is, as we have before said, a part of Christianity; upon its peaceful observance Christianity in a great measure depends for its support. Destroy this day, and a revolution of the most astounding character will be produced. Whatever conclusion may be arrived at upon the evidence submitted in the case before the court, we cannot assert as law a principle which must lead to the most disastrous results, which must shake Christianity itself; which Christianity, in the expressive language of Judge Duncan, 'is not proclaimed by the commanding voice of any human superior, but expressed in the calm and mild accents of customary law. Its foundations are broad, and strong, and deep; they are laid in the authority, the interests and the affections of the people. Waiving all questions of hereafter, it is the purest system of morality, the firmest auxiliary, and only stable support of all human laws.' "

It is the right, then, of the State to protect by law such a fundamental support of government. This attack on the Sabbath is treason against the very foundations of government. As such, let it be resisted by every American citizen. The American Sabbath is essential to American liberty, to our republic, and to God's religion.

THE END.